THE HAWTHORN SERIES

Classic
Essential

SOUPS

CONFIDENT COOKING

Your Promise of Success

Welcome to the world of Confident Cooking, created for you in our test
kitchen, where recipes are double-tested by our team of home
economists to achieve a high standard of success.

MURDOCH BOOKS®
Sydney • London • Vancouver • New York

3.75

~ Pumpkin Soup ~

Preparation time:
25 minutes
Total cooking time:
35 minutes

Serves 4–6

1 kg pumpkin	salt and pepper, to taste
60 g butter	3/4 cup cream
1 onion, chopped	shredded fresh basil, to
4 cups chicken stock	serve

1 ~Peel pumpkin and chop into medium-sized pieces. Heat butter in a medium pan; add onion, cook gently 15 minutes until onion is soft.
2 ~Add pumpkin and stock. Simmer, covered, for 20 minutes, or until pumpkin is tender. Cool.

3 ~In food processor or blender, process mixture in batches until smooth. Return to pan.
4 ~Add salt and pepper to taste; stir in cream. Stir over low heat to heat through. Top with fresh basil just before serving, if desired.
Note ~When pureeing hot soup, process in small batches only.

Over-filling the food processor or blender can be hazardous, causing hot liquid to overflow onto hands or bench.
Omit cream from this recipe if you prefer a thicker, non-dairy soup. Butternut pumpkin may be used. It is easier to peel and can also be used unpeeled—the skin softens with cooking.

Roughly chop the peeled pumpkin into medium-sized pieces.

Add the pumpkin pieces and chicken stock to onion in the pan.

Process the pumpkin mixture in a food processor until smooth.

Add the cream and stir soup over low heat until heated through.

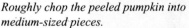

～ Dutch Pea and Ham Soup ～

Preparation time:
20 minutes + several hours or overnight soaking
Total cooking time:
2¹/₂ hours

Serves 4–6

---

2 cups green split peas
750 g ham bones
10 cups (2¹/₂ litres) water
1 stick celery, including tops, chopped
1 carrot, chopped
1 onion, chopped
3 leeks, sliced
1 potato, chopped
pork sausage, parsley and rye bread, to serve

---

1 ～Soak split peas in cold water for several hours or overnight. Place bones, drained peas, water, celery, carrot and onion in a large pan. Bring to boil and simmer, covered, for 2 hours, or until the peas are tender.

2 ～Add leek and potato; cook for another 30 minutes, or until vegetables are tender.

3 ～Remove ham bones from pan, chop the meat and return it to pan; discard bones.

4 ～Cool mixture slightly; push through a sieve. Return to pan and heat through. Top with sliced pork sausage and a sprig of parsley. Serve with rye bread.

Note ～If a chunkier soup is preferred, the sieving can be omitted.

Place bones, soaked peas, celery, carrot and onion in a large pan with the water.

Add sliced leek and the chopped potato to the pan when peas are tender.

Finely chop the meat from the ham bones and discard the bones.

Push the soup mixture through a sieve before returning to pan to reheat.

～ Cream of Mushroom Soup ～

Preparation time:
25 minutes
Total cooking time:
15–20 minutes

Serves 4–6

400 g mushrooms	4 cups chicken stock
60 g butter	1 cup cream
3 cloves garlic, crushed	salt and pepper, to taste
1/4 cup plain flour	

1 ～Using your fingers, carefully peel the skin from the mushrooms. Chop the stems and caps coarsely. Heat the butter in a large pan, add the garlic and mushrooms and cook for 5 minutes, or until the mushrooms are soft.

2 ～Add the flour and stir for 1 minute. Stir in the chicken stock and simmer, covered, for 10 minutes.

3 ～In a food processor or blender, process soup in batches until smooth. Return to pan; add the cream and stir over low heat until soup is heated through. Add the salt and pepper and serve.

Note ～Large, flat mushrooms will give a stronger flavour to this soup than the smaller button mushrooms, but either can be used.

～ Vichyssoise ～
(Potato and Leek Soup)

Preparation time:
25 minutes
Total cooking time:
30 minutes

Serves 4–6

60 g butter	1 cup milk
2 medium leeks, chopped	salt and pepper, to taste
2 large potatoes, peeled, chopped	sour cream or cream, for serving
3 cups chicken stock	chives, chopped, for garnish

1 ～Heat butter in a medium pan, add leeks. Cook, stirring, until soft.

2 ～Add the potatoes and stock. Simmer for 15–20 minutes, or until potatoes are tender. Stir in milk. Season with salt and pepper.

3 ～Transfer soup to food processor or blender, process in batches until smooth. If serving soup hot, return to pan and heat through. Refrigerate if serving cold. Spoon sour cream on top and sprinkle with chives before serving.

Note ～Vichyssoise is a classic cream soup which was created by the Ritz-Carlton Hotel in New York. It makes an elegant first course for a dinner party and is traditionally served well chilled, not just at room temperature.

Cream of Mushroom Soup (top) and Vichyssoise

～ Clam Chowder ～

Preparation time:
35 minutes
Total cooking time:
30 minutes

Serves 4

1¹/₂ kg fresh clams in shell (vongole)	500 g potato, peeled and cubed
1 cup water	1¹/₄ cups fish stock
1 tablespoon oil	2 cups milk
125 g bacon, chopped	¹/₂ cup cream
1 onion, chopped	salt and pepper, to taste

1 ～Place clams in large pan with water. Simmer, covered, over low heat 5 minutes, or until shells open (discard unopened ones). Strain liquid, reserve. Remove clam meat from shells, discard shells. Chop meat finely.
2 ～Heat oil in pan, add bacon and onion. Cook, stirring, until bacon is crisp and onion soft. Add potato and stir.
3 ～Measure reserved clam liquid, add water to make 1¹/₄ cups. Add this liquid, stock and milk to pan. Bring to boil, simmer, covered, over low heat for 20 minutes, or until potato is tender.
4 ～Add cream, clam meat, and salt and pepper. Heat through gently before serving.
Note ～Fresh clams, available at fish markets, give the best flavour but canned clams (drained) may be used. Make up liquid with fish stock.

Cook the clams in a large pan of water until the shells open.

Cook chopped bacon and onion in pan until bacon is crisp and onion soft.

Add the clam liquid, fish stock and milk to the bacon, onion and potato.

Add the cream and the chopped clam meat to soup and heat through gently. ·

~ Cream of Asparagus Soup ~

Preparation time:
25 minutes
Total cooking time:
25–30 minutes

Serves 4–6

750 g fresh asparagus spears	**1 celery stick, chopped**
60 g butter	**1/4 cup plain flour**
1 small onion, chopped	**3 cups chicken stock**
	2/3 cup cream

1 ~Cut tips from asparagus spears. Finely chop spears. Drop tips into boiling salted water for 1 minute; drain.

2 ~Heat butter in a large pan, add onion, celery and chopped asparagus spears. Cook for 5 minutes, stirring, until onion is soft. Add flour and stir until combined.

3 ~Remove from heat, add stock, stirring until combined. Return to heat and simmer, covered, 20–25 minutes, or until vegetables are tender. Add tips, simmer for another 5 minutes.

4 ~Transfer mixture to a food processor or blender and process in small batches until smooth. Return to pan; add cream and stir to combine. Stir soup over low heat until heated through. Serve garnished with a sprig of fresh chervil, if desired.

Note ~This soup is equally delicious served chilled as a summer lunch dish.

After cutting off tips, finely chop the asparagus spears.

Cook chopped onion and asparagus until onion is soft.

Add chicken stock to the pan and stir to combine with other ingredients.

Transfer soup mixture to food processor and process in batches until smooth.

~ Tomato Soup ~

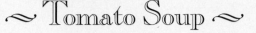

Preparation time:
25 minutes
Total cooking time:
20 minutes

Serves 4–6

1 ~Mark a small cross in the base of each tomato. Place tomatoes in boiling water for 1–2 minutes, then plunge into cold water. Peel skin of each tomato downwards away from the cross. Chop flesh. Heat oil in a medium

1 kg tomatoes	1 tablespoon tomato paste
1 tablespoon oil	4 cups chicken stock
1 onion, chopped	salt and pepper, to taste
2 cloves garlic, crushed	1/2 teaspoon sugar

pan, add the onion and garlic. Cook 5 minutes, or until onion is tender.
2 ~Add tomato and tomato paste; simmer, covered, for 10 minutes.
3 ~Add stock, salt and pepper, and sugar. Simmer, covered, for another 5 minutes.
4 ~In a food processor or blender, process the

soup in batches until mixture is smooth. Return soup to pan and heat through. Serve garnished with a sprig of fresh chervil, if desired.
Note ~To make Cream of Tomato Soup, add 1/2 cup of cream to soup in pan and heat gently over low heat— do not boil.

~ Chicken Noodle Soup ~

Preparation time:
20 minutes
Total cooking time:
20–25 minutes

Serves 4–6

1 ~Place stock in pan and bring to boil.
2 ~Add shredded chicken. Just before serving, add the noodles and parsley to pan and simmer over low heat for 10–15 minutes, or until noodles are tender. Add pepper and serve.

8 cups chicken stock	3/4 cup chopped fresh parsley
1 cup finely shredded cooked chicken	pepper to taste
1 cup broken thin noodles	

Note ~Noodles must be added close to serving time, otherwise they will soften too much on standing. Omit shredded chicken if a less substantial Chicken Noodle Soup is desired. If chicken stock is unavailable, use 8 cups water with 1 tablespoon chicken stock powder.

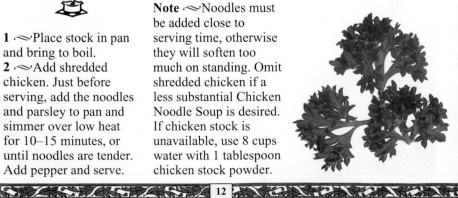

Tomato Soup (top) and Chicken Noodle Soup

~ Chicken and Corn Soup ~

Preparation time:
25 minutes
Total cooking time:
20 minutes

Serves 4–6

2 cm piece fresh ginger, peeled	1/4 cup cornflour
4 corn cobs	1/3 cup water
6 cups chicken stock	8 spring onions, finely
1 cup shredded cooked chicken	chopped
	1/2 teaspoon sesame oil
	salt and pepper

1 ~ Finely grate the fresh ginger.
2 ~ Steam corn cobs until tender. Cool, then cut corn kernels from cobs. Heat the stock in a medium pan and add the corn, chicken and ginger. Simmer mixture, uncovered, 5 minutes.

3 ~ Combine cornflour and water in a small bowl and mix to a smooth paste. Add to the pan, stirring until soup mixture thickens.
4 ~ Add spring onion and sesame oil and stir to combine. Add salt and pepper to taste. Serve immediately.

Note ~ For a creamier consistency, puree half the cooked kernels in a food processor before adding. Canned corn niblets or creamed corn can also be used. For Sweet Corn and Crab Meat soup, replace the chicken with shredded crab meat.

Grate the peeled piece of fresh ginger on a fine grater.

Cut the kernels from the cooked corn cobs, using a sharp knife.

Add the cornflour and water paste to the soup mixture in pan.

Stir in the spring onion, sesame oil, and salt and pepper.

~ Borscht ~
(Cold Beetroot Soup)

Preparation time:
30 minutes
Total cooking time:
40 minutes

Serves 6

6 large (1¹/₂ kg) beetroot, peeled	**6 teaspoons caster sugar**
9 cups (2¹/₄ litres) water	**¹/₂ cup lemon juice**
	3 eggs
	salt and pepper

1 ~Grate beetroot. Place the beetroot, water and sugar in a pan and stir over low heat until sugar has dissolved. Simmer, partially covered, for 30 minutes, skimming surface occasionally.

2 ~Add lemon juice and simmer, uncovered, for 10 minutes. Remove pan from heat.
3. ~Whisk eggs in a bowl. Gradually pour eggs into the beetroot mixture, whisking constantly and taking care not to curdle the eggs. Add salt and

pepper. Cool soup, then cover and refrigerate until cold. Serve Borscht topped with a dollop of sour cream, if desired.
Note ~For a hot, hearty version of this traditional eastern European dish, see recipe for Hot Beef Borscht on page 32.

~ Cold Cucumber Soup ~

Preparation time:
20 minutes
Total cooking time:
Nil

Serves 4–6

1 large green cucumber	**1¹/₃ cups cream**
1 large dill pickle, chopped	**1¹/₄ cups chicken stock**
2 tablespoons lemon juice	**salt and pepper, to taste**
¹/₂ onion, grated	**1 tablespoon chopped fresh dill**

1 ~ Peel, seed and chop cucumber, leaving a small amount for garnish, if desired. Place remaining cucumber, dill pickle, lemon juice and onion in food processor. Process until smooth and fine.
2 ~Transfer mixture to

a large bowl, stir in the cream, stock, and salt and pepper to taste. Add dill and stir until combined. Refrigerate. Serve with reserved cucumber and an extra sprinkling of dill, if desired.
Note ~The easiest way to seed a cucumber is to

cut it in half lengthways and scoop out the seeds with a teaspoon.
  Cucumber Soup is best served a day or two after being made, to allow the flavour to develop fully. Yoghurt (low fat if you prefer) can be substituted for the cream, if desired.

Borscht (top) and Cold Cucumber Soup

～ Minestrone ～
(Italian Vegetable Soup)

Preparation time:
30 minutes + overnight soaking
Total cooking time:
2³/4 hours

Serves 6–8

250 g haricot beans	1 turnip, chopped
2 tablespoons oil	2 potatoes, chopped
2 onions, chopped	1 stick celery, chopped
2 cloves garlic, crushed	1/4 cup tomato paste
2 rashers bacon, chopped	1 zucchini, sliced
4 tomatoes, peeled and chopped	1/2 cup green beans
1/4 cup chopped parsley	1/2 cup macaroni elbows
9 cups beef stock	1/4 cup grated cheddar cheese
1/4 cup red wine	salt, pepper
1 carrot, chopped	shaved parmesan cheese, to serve

1 ～Soak haricot beans overnight in water; drain. Add to pan of boiling water, simmer 15 minutes; drain. Heat oil in pan, add onion, garlic and bacon. Cook, stirring, until onion is soft and bacon crisp.

2 ～Add tomato, parsley, haricot beans, stock and wine. Simmer, covered, over low heat 2 hours.
3 ～Add carrot, turnip, potato, celery and tomato paste; simmer, covered, 15–20 minutes.
4 ～Just before serving, add zucchini, green beans, macaroni and cheese. Simmer, covered, 10–15 minutes, or until vegetables and pasta are tender. Season with salt and pepper.

Serve topped with shavings of parmesan cheese.
Note ～If you prefer, the pasta may be cooked separately in boiling water and added to the soup just before serving.

Minestrone makes a substantial meal in itself, served with fresh crusty bread. For a lighter version, use chicken stock instead of the beef stock and omit the bacon.

Drain haricot beans after soaking them overnight in water.

Add tomato and parsley to the bacon, onion and garlic mixture.

Add the tomato paste and remaining vegetables to pan.

Simmer soup until the vegetables and pasta are tender.

∼ Cream of Cauliflower Soup ∼

Preparation time:
20 minutes
Total cooking time:
15–20 minutes

Serves 4–6

750 g cauliflower	**¹/₄ teaspoon ground**
1 tablespoon oil	**nutmeg**
3 cups chicken stock	**salt and pepper, to taste**
1 cup cream	

1 ∼Cut cauliflower into small florets. Heat oil in a large pan; add cauliflower and stir-fry for 3 minutes, or until just starting to soften.
2 ∼Add stock; simmer, covered, 10–15 minutes or until cauliflower is tender. Stir in cream.

3 ∼In a food processor or blender, process soup in batches until smooth. Return soup to the pan. Add nutmeg, and salt and pepper to taste. Heat through gently and serve immediately, sprinkled with freshly ground pepper, if desired.
Note ∼This soup has a deliciously delicate flavour and texture.

Even those who dislike eating cauliflower as a vegetable will usually enjoy it. Choose very fresh cauliflower with a firm head and no brown or black spots.
For an even richer soup, add 1 cup grated cheddar cheese. Garnish with tiny cauliflower florets, or a sprig of fresh chervil.

∼ Cream of Spinach Soup ∼

Preparation time:
25 minutes
Total cooking time:
25 minutes

Serves 4–6

500 g (2 bunches)	**2¹/₂ cups chicken or**
English spinach	**vegetable stock**
60 g butter	**1¹/₂ cups milk**
1 onion, sliced	**¹/₄ teaspoon ground**
2 tablespoons plain	**nutmeg**
flour	**salt and pepper to taste**

1 ∼Trim leaves from stems of spinach; wash leaves, then chop or shred them. Heat butter in a large pan; add onion, cook until soft. Add spinach leaves and cook, stirring, until leaves have wilted and are tender.

2 ∼Add flour, stir over heat until vegetables are coated. Remove mixture from heat, stir in stock; return to heat. Stir over heat until mixture boils and thickens. Add milk, nutmeg, and salt and pepper. Cover, simmer for 15–20 minutes, or until spinach is soft.

3 ∼Cool soup slightly; process in batches in food processor or blender until smooth. Return to pan and heat through. Serve with croûtons, if desired.
Note ∼For a darker soup, replace 1 bunch of the spinach with 1 bunch of silverbeet.

Cream of Cauliflower Soup (top) and Cream of Spinach Soup

~ Beef Consommé ~

Preparation time:
20 minutes
Total cooking time:
45 minutes

Serves 4

350 g gravy beef	1¹/₂ litres beef stock
2 medium carrots	salt and pepper
2 sticks celery	1 medium carrot, extra,
2 small leeks	cut into fine strips
2 medium tomatoes,	1 small leek, extra, cut
roughly chopped	into fine strips
3 egg whites	

1 ～Trim meat of excess fat. Chop meat finely, or mince in a food processor. Finely chop the carrots, celery and leeks. Place in a large pan with tomato, meat and egg whites; mix thoroughly.

2 ～Heat stock until just warm; season with salt and pepper to taste.

Gradually add stock to the meat and vegetable mixture, whisking continuously over medium heat. Continue whisking for about 10 minutes, bringing mixture slowly to boil. Reduce heat. Using a large spoon, make a hole in layer of froth floating on top of stock. Simmer gently, uncovered, for 35 minutes; do not stir. Place a damp tea-towel or a double layer of fine muslin into a large strainer. Strain the liquid into a large, clean pan. Taste and add extra salt, if desired. Reheat and serve. Garnish with fine

strips of carrot and leek (added at the last minute so as not to cloud the consommé).

Note ～Consommé is a a very clear but strongly flavoured broth which makes a light and elegant start to a dinner party. It is used instead of plain beef stock as the basis of many classic special occasion soups, such as Madrilène (flavoured with celery and tomato) and Longchamps (which has fine noodles, chervil and strips of sorrel added). For an extra clear consommé, the straining may be done twice.

Finely chop the meat, and the carrots, celery and leeks.

Make a hole, with a large spoon, in layer of froth floating on top of stock.

～ Gazpacho ～
(Spanish Cold Tomato and Cucumber Soup)

Preparation time:
20 minutes
Total cooking time:
10–15 minutes

Serves 6–8

1 red onion	salt and pepper to taste
3 tomatoes	1/4 cup olive oil
1/2 medium cucumber	1/4 cup white wine
1/2 green capsicum,	vinegar
seeded	
1/2 red capsicum, seeded	*Garlic Croûtons*
1 clove garlic, crushed	6 slices white bread
850 ml (3 1/2 cups)	1/4 cup olive oil
tomato juice	1 clove garlic, crushed
1/2 teaspoon sugar	

1 ～Finely chop onion, tomatoes, cucumber and capsicum. Place in large bowl with the garlic.

2 ～Stir in juice, sugar, salt and pepper, and combined oil and vinegar. Mix well. Refrigerate. Serve cold, with Garlic Croûtons.

3 ～ **To make Garlic Croûtons:** Preheat oven to moderate 180°C. Trim crusts from bread, cut bread into 1 cm cubes. Drizzle with combined oil and garlic, mix well. Spread on baking tray.

4 ～ Bake for 10–15 minutes, turning twice, or until golden brown.

Chop the onion, tomato, cucumber and capsicum finely.

Add the combined oil and vinegar to tomato juice, vegetables and seasonings.

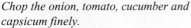

After removing crusts from bread slices, cut bread into small cubes.

Bake Garlic Croûtons in a moderate 180°C oven until golden brown.

～ Lentil and Bacon Soup ～

Preparation time:
25 minutes
Total cooking time:
1 hour 20 minutes

Serves 6

1 cup (200 g) red lentils	salt and pepper, to taste
4¹/2 cups chicken stock	450 g potatoes, peeled
1 clove garlic, crushed	and chopped
2 whole cloves	2 tablespoons lemon
2 bacon rashers,	juice
chopped	1 stick cabanossi, or
410 g can tomatoes, or	2 rashers bacon,
3 tomatoes, chopped	chopped, then fried
1 medium onion,	until crisp, for garnish
chopped	

1 ～Wash the lentils thoroughly; drain well. Place in pan with stock, garlic, cloves, bacon, tomato, onion, and salt and pepper. Bring to boil, reduce heat; simmer, covered, 45 minutes, or until lentils and vegetables are tender.
2 ～Add potato and simmer, covered, for 20 minutes, or until the potato is soft.
3 ～Allow soup to cool slightly; strain through a sieve into a large bowl.
4 ～Return soup to pan. Add the lemon juice and heat through gently. Serve soup topped with chopped or crumbled crisp-fried bacon, or slices of cabanossi.
Note ～Lentil and Bacon Soup can be processed, unstrained, in a food processor or blender, if desired. This makes a heartier soup.

～ Cream of Celery Soup ～

Preparation time:
10 minutes
Total cooking time:
30 minutes

Serves 4–6

1 bunch celery (with	4¹/2 cups chicken stock
leaves)	1¹/2 cups cream
60 g butter	celery salt and pepper
1 onion, chopped	to taste

1 ～Chop the celery finely. Heat butter in pan, add the onion and stir until softened. Add celery and cook, stirring, over low heat until celery is softened but not browned.
2 ～Add stock and simmer, covered, over low heat for 20 minutes, or until celery is tender.
3 ～Blend or process mixture in small batches until smooth. Return to pan, stir in cream and add salt and pepper to taste. Stir soup over heat until just heated through. Serve soup immediately, garnished with celery leaves, if desired.
Note ～Celery must be thoroughly cooked before pureeing; any stringiness will make the soup coarse in texture.

For a delicious variation, crumble some stilton cheese over soup.

Lentil and Bacon Soup (top) and Cream of Celery Soup

~ French Onion Soup ~

Preparation time:
15 minutes
Total cooking time:
1 hour and 15 minutes

Serves 4–6

6 onions (about 1 kg)	salt and pepper
60 g butter	1 stick French bread
1 teaspoon sugar	¹/₂ cup grated gruyère
¹/₄ cup plain flour	or cheddar cheese
9 cups (2¹/₄ litres) beef	grated gruyère cheese,
stock	for serving

1 ~Peel onions and slice into fine rings. Heat butter in large pan, add onion and cook slowly over low heat for about 20 minutes, or until very tender.
2 ~Add the sugar and flour and cook, stirring, for another 1–2 minutes until mixture is just starting to turn golden.
3 ~Stir in stock and simmer, covered, over low heat for 1 hour. Season soup with salt and pepper.
4 ~Preheat oven to 180°C. Cut bread stick into 1.5 cm slices. Bake for 20 minutes, turning once, until slices are dry and lightly golden. Top each slice with some of the grated cheese and place under a hot grill until cheese has melted. Serve French Onion Soup topped with toasted cheese croûtes. Sprinkle with extra grated gruyère cheese.

Peel the onions and slice them carefully into fine rings.

Add the sugar and flour to the softened onions in pan.

Season cooked soup with salt and pepper according to taste.

Place some grated gruyère or cheddar cheese on top of each bread slice.

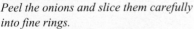

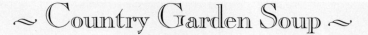

~ Country Garden Soup ~

Preparation time:
35 minutes
Total cooking time:
3 hours

Serves 6–8

2 corn cobs	¹/₂ cup pearl barley
2 tablespoons oil	2 carrots, chopped
600 g beef bones	2 sticks celery, chopped
500 g chuck steak, cubed	2 potatoes, peeled and chopped
10 cups (2¹/₂ litres) water	1 turnip, peeled and chopped
2 bay leaves	3 tomatoes, peeled and chopped
5 whole black peppercorns	1 cup green peas
1 onion, chopped	

1 ⁓Cut corn from cobs. Heat oil in large pan, add beef bones and steak and cook, stirring, until browned. Add water, bay leaves, peppercorns and onion; simmer, covered, over low heat for 2 hours.
2 ⁓Remove bones; skim scum or fat from surface. Add barley; simmer, covered, over low heat for 40 minutes.
3 ⁓Add carrot, celery, potato, turnip and tomato. Simmer, covered, over low heat for 35 minutes, or until vegetables are tender. Add the peas and corn and simmer, covered, until tender.

Add water, seasonings and onion to beef bones and meat in pan.

Remove any scum or fat from the surface of soup with a large spoon.

Add the chopped carrot, celery, potato, turnip and tomato to soup.

Stir in the peas and corn and simmer until all the vegetables are tender.

∼ Hot Beef Borscht ∼

Preparation time:
30 minutes
Total cooking time:
1½ hours

Serves 6–8

1 bunch (600 g) beetroot	500 g tomatoes, peeled and chopped
1 kg chuck steak	1 onion, chopped
2 tablespoons oil	4 cloves garlic, crushed
8 cups water or beef stock	2 potatoes, peeled and chopped
½ small cabbage, shredded	salt and pepper

1 ∼Peel beetroot, cut into 1 cm cubes. Cut meat into small cubes. Heat oil in a large pan, add meat and cook, stirring, until browned.
2 ∼Add water or stock and simmer, covered, for 40 minutes.

3 ∼Add the beetroot, cabbage, tomato, onion and garlic and simmer, covered, for 40 minutes. Add potato and simmer, covered, for 15 minutes or until potato is tender. Season with salt and pepper and serve.

Note ∼Borscht can be served hot or cold (see recipe for cold version on page 16). Sour cream is the traditional topping for this soup, which is favourite fare during bitterly cold eastern European winters.

∼ Cream of Chicken Soup ∼

Preparation time:
15 minutes
Total cooking time:
20 minutes

Serves 4–6

60 g butter	1 cup cream
⅓ cup plain flour	1 stick celery, finely chopped
2 cups chicken stock	salt
1 cup milk	⅓ cup chopped fresh parsley
1 chicken breast fillet, finely chopped	

1 ∼Melt butter in large pan and add the flour. Stir over low heat for 2 minutes, or until lightly golden. Add stock gradually to pan, stirring between each addition until mixture is smooth. Stir constantly over medium heat until the mixture boils and thickens.
2 ∼Add the milk, chicken, cream and celery. Simmer over low heat for 5 minutes, until chicken is tender. Add salt to taste.
3 ∼Serve soup sprinkled with chopped fresh parsley.

Hot Beef Borscht (top) and Cream of Chicken Soup

~ Bouillabaisse ~
(Mediterranean Fisherman's Soup)

Preparation time:
40 minutes
Total cooking time:
1 hour 30 minutes

Serves 4–6

Rouille
**4 thick slices white
  bread, crusts removed**
water for soaking
4 cloves garlic, crushed
**2 red chillies, finely
  chopped**
2 egg yolks
**salt and freshly ground
  black pepper**
3/4 cup olive oil

1–2 fish heads
**500 g green king
  prawns, peeled and
  deveined, shells and
  heads retained**
**1 lobster tail, chop meat
  and retain shell**
1 cup white wine
2 cups water
**1 small red onion,
  chopped**
2 cloves garlic, chopped
1 bay leaf

1/4 cup olive oil
**1 small leek, finely
  sliced**
**2 medium red onions,
  finely chopped, extra**
**4 cloves garlic, extra,
  crushed**
**4–6 tomatoes, skinned
  and chopped**
1/4 cup tomato paste
**1/4 teaspoon saffron
  powder or colour**
2 bay leaves, extra
**1 teaspoon dried basil
  leaves**
1 teaspoon fennel seeds
5 cm piece orange rind
salt and black pepper
**500 g white fleshed fish,
  skinned and boned,
  cut into 3 cm pieces**
**12 mussels, beards
  removed and soaked**
**1/2 cup fresh parsley,
  finely chopped**

1 ~**To make Rouille:**
In a small bowl, place
bread and enough water
to soak. Leave 5 minutes;
squeeze water from
bread and place bread in
food processor with
garlic, chillies, yolks,
salt and pepper. Process
20 seconds. With motor
running, add oil in slow,
steady stream. Transfer
to a serving bowl, cover
and refrigerate.
2 ~**To make
Bouillabaisse:** Place
fish heads with prawn
and lobster shells in a
large pan. Add wine,
water, onion, garlic and
bay leaf. Bring to boil,
simmer 20 minutes.
Strain, reserve liquid.
3 ~Heat oil in large
pan. Add leek, extra
onion, and garlic. Cover
and cook, stirring
occasionally, over low
heat 20 minutes, or until
softened but not browned.
Add tomato, tomato
paste, saffron, bay leaves,
basil, fennel seeds, rind,

salt and pepper; stir
well. Remove lid and
continue to cook for
another 10 minutes,
stirring frequently. Add
reserved fish stock, bring
to boil; boil 10 minutes,
stirring often.
4 ~Lower heat, add
fish, lobster meat and
mussels. Cover and
simmer 4–5 minutes
until mussels have
opened (discard any
unopened mussels). Add

prawns and simmer,
covered, 3–4 minutes or
until just cooked.
Discard rind and bay
leaves. Sprinkle with
parsley. Serve with
French bread and
spoonfuls of Rouille.
Note ~This soup can
be prepared to the end of
step 3 and refrigerated.
Continue with remaining
steps—final cooking
should take no more
than 10–12 minutes.

For the Rouille, pour in olive oil in a slow, steady stream, with motor still running.

Add the fish, lobster flesh and mussels to other ingredients in pan.

Chilled Avocado Soup

Preparation time:
10 minutes
Total cooking time:
Nil

Serves 4–6

3 medium ripe avocados	1/3 cup lemon juice
1 cup cream	sour cream or cream
3 cups chicken stock	and chives or sliced
salt and pepper to taste	spring onions, to serve

1 ⮡Remove skin and seeds from avocados. Process the flesh in a food processor or blender until smooth. Add the cream and process, using pulse button, for several seconds or until mixture is just smooth.

2 ⮡Add stock, salt and pepper to taste, and lemon juice. Process until mixture is just smooth. Serve chilled or at room temperature, topped with a dollop of sour cream or cream and some chopped chives or sliced spring onions. If you wish to serve warm, heat gently.

Note ⮡Avocado Soup should be served as soon as possible after being made. Even though this recipe contains lemon juice, the soup will eventually discolour.

Two sliced spring onions, or 1/4 cup chopped chives, can be added with the stock, if desired.

Carrot Soup

Preparation time:
20 minutes
Total cooking time:
30 minutes

Serves 4–6

500 g carrots	5 cups chicken stock
1 large onion	3/4 cup cream
60 g butter	salt and pepper
1 tablespoon plain flour	chives, to serve

1 ⮡Peel carrots; cut carrots and onion into thin slices. Heat butter in large pan, add onion and carrot; stir over low heat until onion is tender.
2 ⮡Add flour and stir until combined; remove from heat. Add the stock, stirring until combined. Stir over heat until the mixture boils and thickens. Simmer, covered, over low heat for 25 minutes, or until the carrot is tender.
3 ⮡Use a food processor or blender to process soup in small batches until smooth. Return soup to pan, stir in the cream and season with salt and pepper. Stir until heated through. Serve Carrot Soup sprinkled with chopped chives.
Note ⮡To make Carrot and Orange Soup, stir in the finely grated rind of 1 orange and the juice of 2 oranges. Add a little grated fresh ginger, if desired. Garnish with thin slices of orange or fine strips of rind.

Chilled Avocado Soup (top) and Carrot Soup

～ Mulligatawny ～
(Curry Soup)

Preparation time:
40 minutes
Total cooking time:
1 hour 20 minutes

Serves 6

1 kg chicken pieces
2 tablespoons plain
    flour
2 teaspoons curry
    powder
1 teaspoon turmeric
1/2 teaspoon ground
    ginger
60 g butter
6 whole cloves
12 black peppercorns
1 large apple, peeled
    and chopped
6 cups chicken stock
2 tablespoons lemon
    juice
1/2 cup fresh cream
boiled rice and chutney,
    to serve

1 ～Trim chicken of excess fat and sinew. Combine flour, curry powder, turmeric and ginger; rub into chicken.
2 ～Heat butter in a large pan and cook chicken on all sides until lightly browned. Tie cloves and peppercorns in small piece of muslin, add to pan with stock. Bring to boil, reduce heat slightly and simmer, covered, for 1 hour.
3 ～Remove chicken from pan and discard muslin bag. Remove skin from chicken, finely chop flesh. Skim fat from soup.

4 ～Return chicken meat to pan. Stir in lemon juice and cream; heat through gently. Serve with hot boiled rice and chutney, offered separately.
Note ～Mulligatawny was a favourite Anglo-Indian dish (the name comes from a Tamil word meaning 'pepper water'). It is not meant to be as hot as a curry, but the amount of curry powder can be varied if you prefer. For a lighter soup, the chicken flesh

may be omitted. Coconut cream can be substituted for the cream; do not allow the soup to boil after adding or it will curdle.

Rub flour and spice mixture into the chicken pieces.

Add cloves and peppercorns, tied in muslin, to the pan.

*Finely chop the cooked chicken flesh
before returning to pan.*

*Stir in lemon juice and cream and heat
through gently.*

~ Prawn Bisque ~

Preparation time:
25 minutes
Total cooking time:
15–20 minutes

Serves 4–6

500 g green prawns	**¹/₂ teaspoon paprika**
60 g butter	**salt to taste**
2 tablespoons plain flour	**1 cup cream**
	¹/₃ cup dry sherry
8 cups fish stock	**paprika, extra, to serve**

1 ⁓Shell and devein prawns, reserving heads and shells. Heat butter in pan, add heads and shells; cook 5 minutes, crushing heads with a wooden spoon.
2 ⁓Add the flour and stir until combined. Add stock, paprika and salt.

Stir over heat until the mixture boils. Simmer, covered, over low heat for 10 minutes. Strain mixture, add prawns. Cook 2–3 minutes. Cool slightly, then place in batches in blender or food processor and process until smooth.
3 ⁓Return mixture to pan. Add cream and

sherry and stir. Heat through before serving. Serve sprinkled with paprika.
Note ⁓The prawn heads and shells are what give Prawn Bisque its rich, concentrated flavour. A few small cooked prawns may be reserved for garnishing, if desired.

~ Miso Soup ~

Preparation time:
30 minutes
Total cooking time:
5 minutes

Serves 4

20 g wakame (dried seaweed)	**250 g tofu, cubed**
3 cups dashi (Japanese stock)	**2 tablespoons red miso**

1 ⁓Rinse wakame, place in a small bowl and cover with water. Leave to soak for 15 minutes, drain and cut into small pieces.
2 ⁓Place dashi in a medium pan and bring to the boil. Add wakame

and tofu, then reduce heat and simmer for 1 minute.
3 ⁓Place the miso in a small bowl, add a little hot dashi and stir until miso has dissolved. Remove pan from heat. Add miso mixture to pan, stir to combine. Serve immediately.
Note ⁓Ingredients for Miso Soup can be found

in Asian supermarkets and in most health food stores. Dashi is the basic stock used in Japanese cooking and is made by boiling dried kelp and dried bonito (small fish). You can make your own, but instant dashi powder sold in packets is more convenient. Add hot water to make up into stock.

Prawn Bisque (top) and Miso Soup

~ Szechwan Soup ~
(Hot and Sour Soup)

Preparation time:
**20 minutes + 30
minutes soaking**
Total cooking time:
15 minutes

Serves 6–8

1 ~Place Chinese
mushrooms in a bowl
and cover with hot
water. Soak mushrooms
30 minutes, drain them
thoroughly and chop.
Soak cellophane
noodles in cold water
20 minutes; drain the
noodles and cut them
into short lengths.

4 dried Chinese mushrooms	1 tablespoon cornflour
45 g wide cellophane noodles	1/3 cup water
4 cups chicken stock	1 egg, lightly beaten
1 cup chopped cooked chicken	1 tablespoon tomato sauce
230 g can bamboo shoots, drained and chopped	1 tablespoon soy sauce
	1 tablespoon vinegar
	2 teaspoons sesame oil
	2 spring onions, finely chopped
1 teaspoon grated fresh ginger	salt and black pepper

2 ~Heat the stock in a
large pan and bring to
the boil. Add the
mushrooms, noodles,
chicken, bamboo shoots
and ginger. Reduce heat
and simmer gently.

3 ~Combine the
cornflour and water in a
small bowl; mix to a
smooth paste. Add
mixture to the soup and
stir until clear. Add the
beaten egg to the soup in
a fine stream, stirring
mixture constantly.

4 ~Remove pan from
heat. Add tomato sauce,
soy sauce, vinegar,
sesame oil and spring
onions. Season with salt
and pepper to taste.
Serve soup topped with
extra spring onions, if
desired.

Note ~Szechwan is a
Chinese regional style of
cooking known for its
spiciness. Add a few
drops of chilli oil to the
recipe if a more fiery
soup is desired.

*Cut the soaked and drained cellophane
noodles into short lengths.*

*Add bamboo shoots to stock with
mushrooms, noodles, chicken and ginger.*

Pour beaten egg into soup in a thin stream, stirring constantly.

Stir in tomato sauce, soy sauce, vinegar, sesame oil and spring onions.

～ Seafood Laksa ～

Preparation time:
45 minutes
Total cooking time:
35 minutes

Serves 4

1 kg medium green prawns	2 stalks lemon grass, white part only
1/2 cup oil	400 ml can coconut milk or cream
1 litre water	3 teaspoons salt
6 large red chillies, seeded	1 teaspoon soft brown sugar
1 large onion, roughly chopped	125 g rice vermicelli noodles
2 cloves garlic, peeled	2 small Lebanese cucumbers
3 slices ginger or galangal	250 g fresh bean sprouts
1 teaspoon turmeric	1/3 cup chopped fresh mint, or Vietnamese mint sprigs, to serve
1 tablespoon ground coriander	
6 macadamia nuts, optional	
1 teaspoon shrimp paste	

1 ～Peel and devein prawns, leaving tails intact. Reserve heads and shells. Heat 2 tablespoons of the oil in a large pan, add the prawn heads and shells. Stir-fry until bright orange; add water. Bring to boil, reduce heat and simmer for 15 minutes. Strain, discard shells.

2 ～Place chillies, onion, garlic, ginger, turmeric, coriander and nuts in food processor. Process until smooth, adding a little water if necessary. Heat the remaining oil in a large pan, add onion mixture and shrimp paste.

Flatten lemon grass with a heavy knife, add to pan. Stir over low heat 3 minutes, until fragrant.

3 ～Add prawn stock, simmer 10 minutes. Add coconut milk, salt and sugar; simmer, uncovered, 5 minutes. Add prawns, cook for 2 minutes until just pink. Remove with a slotted spoon; set aside.

4 ～Bring a pan of water to the boil, add noodles, cook 2 minutes; drain. Cut cucumbers into thin 5 cm lengths. Remove tails from bean sprouts. Place noodles in large tureen, top with cucumber, bean sprouts and prawns. Pour hot soup over. Sprinkle with chopped mint to serve.

After stir-frying prawn heads and shells, add water to pan.

Add bruised lemon grass stalk to shrimp paste and spicy onion mixture in pan.

Remove the cooked prawns with a slotted spoon and set aside.

Remove the tails from the bean sprouts before placing in tureen.

~ Scotch Broth ~

Preparation time:
**30 minutes +
refrigeration**
Total cooking time:
2³/4 hours

Serves 6–8

1 kg lamb neck chops or shanks	1 turnip, chopped
10 cups water or stock	1 onion, chopped
salt and pepper to taste	2 leeks, sliced
1 carrot, chopped	¹/2 cup pearl barley
	¹/2 cup chopped parsley

1 ~Trim fat from the chops. Place meat in a large saucepan with the water, and salt and pepper. Bring to the boil and simmer, covered, for 1 hour, skimming scum from the surface of soup occasionally.

2 ~Add carrot, turnip, onion, leek and barley; simmer, covered, for another 1–1¹/2 hours, or until vegetables and barley are tender. Remove the meat from bones and return it to the pan. Cool to room temperature, then refrigerate until cold. Just before serving,

remove the solidified fat from top. Heat through and stir in parsley. Serve with thick, crusty bread, if desired.
Note ~This soup, also known as barley broth, should be thick and filling, almost like a vegetable stew. Other vegetables in season may be used.

~ Potage Bonne Femme ~
(Potato and Carrot Soup)

Preparation time:
20 minutes
Total cooking time:
40–50 minutes

Serves 6–8

500 g potatoes	1 teaspoon sugar
3 carrots	salt and pepper
2 leeks	³/4 cup cream
30 g butter	parsley or chervil, to
6 cups water or chicken stock	serve

1 ~Peel the potatoes and carrots. Chop potatoes, carrot and leeks into pieces. Heat the butter in a large pan, add leek and carrot; cook, stirring until soft. Add potato and stir to coat with butter.

2 ~Add water or stock, sugar, and salt and pepper. Cover and simmer 30–40 minutes, or until the vegetables are tender.
3 ~Place vegetables in food processor, process in batches until smooth. Return mixture to pan,

stir in cream. Heat through before serving. Serve soup garnished with parsley or chervil.
Note ~For leek and potato soup, omit the carrot and add an extra leek. Top soup with extra cream before serving, if desired.

Scotch Broth (top) and Potage Bonne Femme

~ Green Spring Soup ~

Preparation time:
30 minutes
Total cooking time:
25 minutes

Serves 6–8

6 spring onions	200 g spinach leaves, shredded
1 tablespoon oil	
450 g potatoes, peeled and chopped	200 g lettuce leaves, shredded
2 carrots, chopped	200 g sorrel leaves, shredded
2 leeks, chopped	
1 tablespoon chopped fresh thyme	250 g watercress, rinsed and chopped
5 cloves garlic, crushed	8 cups vegetable stock or water
1/2 cup chopped fresh parsley	1 cup milk
salt to taste	3 egg yolks
	extra salt and pepper

1 ~ Chop spring onions. Heat oil in a large pan, add the potato, carrot, leek, spring onion, thyme, garlic, parsley and salt.

2 ~ Cook, stirring, over medium heat for 5 minutes or until the vegetables soften. Add spinach, lettuce, sorrel and watercress and stir over heat until the leaves have wilted.

3 ~ Add the vegetable stock or water and simmer for 15 minutes or until the vegetables are tender. Process soup in batches in a food processor or blender until mixture is smooth.

Return soup to the pan, then whisk in the milk and egg yolks. Heat through gently, stirring often. Season soup with extra salt and pepper to taste and serve garnished with fresh herbs, if desired.

Note ~ The addition of egg yolks makes this light vegetable soup more substantial. Serve with a swirl of cream or yoghurt on top, if desired.

For the best flavour, make your own vegetable stock for this soup from a good selection of *fresh* vegetables—leftovers or wilted produce will not give the same result.

Chop the spring onions and other vegetables finely.

Cook the chopped vegetables over medium heat until softened.

Add stock or water to the vegetables and simmer until tender.

Return mixture to pan and whisk in the yolks and milk.

～ Beef Goulash ～

Preparation time:
**20 minutes +
refrigeration**
Total cooking time:
2 hours

Serves 4–6

4 thick rashers bacon or 60 g speck	1 medium tomato, peeled and chopped
60 g butter	2 tablespoons tomato paste
2 onions, chopped	8 cups beef stock
2 cloves garlic, crushed	3 medium potatoes, chopped
6 teaspoons paprika salt to taste	
1 kg chuck steak, cubed	

1 ～Cut bacon into strips, or speck into small cubes. Heat butter in a large pan, add bacon or speck, onion and garlic; cook until onion is soft and bacon crisp.
2 ～Add paprika, salt and steak. Cook, stirring, over heat for 2–3 minutes. Add the tomato, tomato paste and stock. Simmer, covered, 1 1/2–2 hours, or until meat is tender.
3 ～Add potato and cook soup for another 20 minutes, or until the potato is tender. Season with salt and pepper, if desired. Refrigerate overnight. Skim fat from surface, reheat and serve.
Note ～Speck is pork fat with a thin layer of meat. It has a stronger flavour than bacon.

～ Avgolemono ～
(Greek Egg and Lemon Soup)

Preparation time:
20 minutes
Total cooking time:
10 minutes

Serves 4–6

6 cups chicken stock	2 eggs, separated
3/4 cup white, long-grain rice	1/2 cup lemon juice

1 ～Bring stock to boil in a large pan. Add the rice and simmer for 8–10 minutes until tender. Reserve 2 cups hot stock.
2 ～Beat egg whites in small dry mixing bowl until soft peaks form. Add yolks, beat until combined. Gradually pour lemon juice, then stock, into egg mixture, beating constantly. Pour mixture quickly into cooked rice, stir through.
Note ～Egg and Lemon Soup, one of the most renowned dishes of Greek cuisine, can also be made with fish stock. Assemble ingredients and utensils beforehand, work quickly and serve immediately as this soup does not reheat well.

Beef Goulash (top) and Greek Egg and Lemon Soup

~ Chicken Soup with Matzo Balls ~

Preparation time:
40 minutes + 1 hour refrigeration
Total cooking time:
2 hours 30 minutes

Serves 6

Soup	Matzo Balls
1.75 kg chicken	**2 tablespoons chicken**
4 litres water	**fat or vegetable oil**
3 onions, sliced	**1 medium onion, finely**
4 carrots, chopped	**chopped**
4 sticks celery,	**1 cup coarse matzo**
chopped	**meal**
2 large parsley sprigs	**2 eggs, beaten**
1 bay leaf	**1 tablespoon fresh**
8 black peppercorns	**chopped parsley**
1 tablespoon salt	**salt and pepper**
	almond meal

1 ∼Trim excess fat from chicken, reserve fat. Cut chicken into 8 or 9 pieces, place in large pan with water and other soup ingredients. Bring to boil slowly; skim surface. Reduce heat, simmer 2 hours or until chicken is very tender. Strain, return soup to rinsed pan; bring to boil. Remove chicken from bones, reserve chicken.
2 ∼Add Matzo Balls to soup and simmer, uncovered, 15 minutes. Add chicken, simmer another 5–10 minutes.
3 ∼**To make Matzo Balls** ∼Heat fat or oil in pan, cook onion until golden. Transfer to bowl. Add matzo meal, eggs and parsley; season with salt and pepper. Add enough almond meal to bind. Cover and refrigerate 1 hour. Dip hands in cold water, roll mixture into 2 cm balls.

~ Watercress Soup ~

Preparation time:
15 minutes
Total cooking time:
15–20 minutes

Serves 4–6

1 onion	**3 cups chicken stock**
4 spring onions	**1$\frac{1}{4}$ cups water**
450 g watercress	**salt and pepper to taste**
100 g butter	**sour cream or cream to**
$\frac{1}{3}$ cup plain flour	**serve**

1 ∼Roughly chop the onion, spring onions and watercress. Heat the butter in a large pan and add onion, spring onion and watercress. Stir over low heat for 3 minutes or until the vegetables have softened.
2 ∼Add flour and stir until combined. Gradually add the stock and water to pan, stirring until mixture is smooth. Stir until mixture boils and thickens. Simmer, covered, over low heat for 10 minutes or until the watercress is tender. Cool slightly.
3 ∼Transfer mixture to a food processor or

Chicken Soup with Matzo Balls (top) and Watercress Soup

blender, process in batches until smooth. Before serving, gently heat through, season with salt and pepper. Serve with a dollop of sour cream or cream and garnish with fresh watercress, if desired.

~ Stracciatella ~
(Italian Egg Broth)

Preparation time:
15 minutes
Total cooking time:
10 minutes

Serves 4–6

6 cups chicken stock	**3 eggs**
60 g grated fresh parmesan cheese	**¹/₃ cup chopped fresh parsley**

1 ~Place chicken stock in pan and bring to boil.

2 ~In a medium bowl, beat together the parmesan cheese, eggs and parsley. Whisk mixture quickly into the hot chicken stock. Stir over heat 1–2 minutes, or until heated through. Serve Stracciatella topped with extra parsley and parmesan cheese, if desired.

~ Seafood Chowder ~

Preparation time:
15 minutes
Total cooking time:
30 minutes

Makes 10 cups

60 g butter	**400 g firm white fish, skinned, boned and cut into 2 cm cubes**
2 rashers bacon, finely chopped	
1 leek, finely chopped	**250 g scallops, cleaned, deveined and halved**
1 carrot, peeled and finely chopped	
1 celery stick, finely chopped	**200 g small peeled school prawns**
1 large potato, peeled and chopped	**1 cup cream**
¹/₃ cup plain flour	**¹/₃ cup fresh parsley, finely chopped**
4 cups fish stock, hot	**salt and black pepper**

1 ~Heat 30 g butter in a large saucepan, add bacon. Cook over low heat for 5 minutes; remove the bacon and set aside. Add remaining butter, stir in leek, carrot, celery and potato. Cook over medium heat, stirring often, for 5 minutes or until the vegetables soften and are lightly golden.
2 ~Add flour and cook for 1 minute; add heated fish stock all at once. Cook, stirring, 5 minutes or until smooth and thickened. Simmer for 5 minutes, uncovered.
3 ~Add fish pieces; cook 5 minutes, stirring frequently. Add the scallops, prawns, cream, parsley and reserved bacon; mix well. Reheat for 5 minutes without boiling. Add salt and pepper to taste.

Note ~Seafood Chowder may be made several hours ahead, up to step 3. Cook the fish and shellfish just before serving.

It is important to use white-fleshed fish for this soup. Darker-fleshed fish may give the chowder an oily taste and greyish tinge.

Stracciatella (top) and Seafood Chowder

~ Soupe au Pistou ~
(Vegetable Soup with Basil Sauce)

Preparation time:
45 minutes
Total cooking time:
35–40 minutes

Serves 8

1 ~Thinly slice onions and leek. Tie parsley, rosemary, thyme and marjoram together with string. Heat the oil in a heavy-based pan; add onion and leek. Cook over low heat for 10 minutes or until soft.
2 ~Add herb bunch, bay leaf, pumpkin, potato, carrot, zucchini, salt, and water or stock. Cover, simmer 10 minutes, or until vegetables are almost tender.
3 ~Add broad beans, peas, tomato and pasta. Cover and cook for another 15 minutes or until the vegetables are

2 medium onions
1 leek
3 stalks fresh parsley
1 large sprig fresh rosemary
1 large sprig fresh thyme
1 large sprig fresh marjoram
1/4 cup olive oil
1 bay leaf
375 g pumpkin, cut into small pieces
250 g potato, cut into small pieces
1 medium carrot, cut in half lengthways and thinly sliced
2 small zucchini, finely chopped
1 teaspoon salt

8 cups water or vegetable stock
1/2 cup fresh or frozen broad beans
1/2 cup fresh or frozen peas
2 tomatoes, peeled and roughly chopped
1/2 cup short macaroni or shell pasta

Pistou
1/2 cup fresh basil leaves
2 large cloves garlic, crushed
1/2 teaspoon black pepper
1/3 cup grated parmesan cheese
1/3 cup olive oil

very tender and pasta is cooked (add more water if necessary). Remove the herbs, including bay leaf.
4 ~**To make Pistou:** Process basil, garlic, pepper and cheese in food processor for 20 seconds or until finely chopped. Pour in oil gradually, processing until smooth. Refrigerate. Reheat soup and serve Pistou spooned over the top.

Tie together parsley, rosemary, thyme and marjoram with string.

Add water or stock to the pan with the herbs and vegetables.

Cook until the vegetables are tender and pasta is cooked.

To make Pistou, pour the oil gradually into food processor, processing until smooth.

～ Tom Kha Gai ～

(Thai Chicken and Coconut Milk Soup)

Preparation time:
20 minutes
Total cooking time:
10 minutes

Serves 4

2¹/2 cups chicken stock	**2 tablespoons lemon**
2 kaffir lime leaves	**juice**
5 cm piece lemon grass,	**1 chicken breast fillet,**
white part only, finely	**finely sliced**
chopped	**1¹/2 cups coconut milk**
3 cm piece galangal, cut	**2 small red chillies, split**
into 4 long pieces	**fresh coriander, to**
2 tablespoons fish sauce	**serve**

1 ～Heat stock in a medium pan, add lime leaves, lemon grass, galangal, fish sauce and juice. Bring to boil.
2 ～Add chicken and coconut milk. Reduce heat and simmer for 3–5 minutes, stirring, until chicken is cooked. Add the chillies and cook for another minute.
3 ～Ladle the soup into serving bowls and garnish with fresh coriander. Serve.

～ Won ton Soup ～

(Short Soup)

Preparation time:
45 minutes
Total cooking time:
20 minutes

Serves 6

3 dried Chinese	**1 teaspoon grated**
mushrooms	**ginger**
125 g pork mince	**1 tablespoon finely**
60 g raw prawn meat,	**chopped water**
finely chopped	**chestnuts**
¹/2 teaspoon salt	**24 won ton wrappers**
2 teaspoons soy sauce	**5 cups chicken stock**
1 teaspoon sesame oil	**4 spring onions, very**
1 spring onion, finely	**finely sliced, for**
chopped	**garnish**

1 ～Place mushrooms in small bowl; cover with hot water, leave to soak 30 minutes. Drain, squeeze out excess liquid. Remove stems, chop caps finely. Thoroughly combine mushrooms, pork, prawn meat, salt, soy, sesame oil, spring onion, ginger and water chestnuts.
2 ～Working with one wrapper at a time (cover remainder with clean, damp tea towel), place a level teaspoonful of mixture on each wrapper.
3 ～Moisten edges of wrapper, bring sides up to form a pouch. Place on a plate dusted with flour. Cook in batches in large pan of rapidly boiling water 4–5 minutes; remove, drain. Boil stock in another pan. Place won tons in bowls. Garnish with spring onions, pour in hot stock.

Tom Ka Gai (top) and Won ton soup

～ Cock-a-leekie ～
(Scottish Chicken and Leek Soup)

Preparation time:
20 minutes
Total cooking time:
**2¹/₂ hours +
refrigeration**

Serves 4–6

1 boiling chicken	**200 g pitted prunes**
9 cups water	**2 tablespoons rice**
3 large leeks, sliced	**salt and pepper**

1 ～Cut chicken into pieces, discard as much skin and fat as possible. Place chicken pieces in a large pan with the water. Bring to boil, skimming surface often to remove any scum.

2 ～Add leek, prunes, rice, and salt and pepper. Simmer, covered, for 2–2¹/₂ hours, or until the chicken is tender and soup well flavoured. Season with extra salt and pepper, if desired.
3 ～Cool soup slightly, then remove chicken and bones. Shred chicken and return to pan. Refrigerate soup, preferably overnight. Skim the fat from the surface before reheating and serving. (This step is important to ensure soup is not greasy).
Note ～This delicious soup is a specialty of Scotland and is often served at celebratory dinners. It can also be strained and served as a clear broth, if desired.

～ Oxtail Soup ～

Preparation time:
20 minutes
Total cooking time:
3–3¹/₂ hours

Serves 6–8

1 kg oxtail, sliced	**salt**
60 g butter	**6 black peppercorns**
3 bacon bones	**2 onions, chopped**
1 carrot, chopped	**2 sticks celery, chopped**
1 bay leaf	**2 potatoes, peeled and**
¹/₄ cup parsley sprigs	** chopped**
8 cups water or beef	**1 cup pearl barley**
** stock**	

1 ～Trim excess fat from oxtail, wash well. Heat the butter in a large pan. Add oxtail, bacon bones, carrot, bay leaf and parsley. Stir over heat until bones are lightly browned.
2 ～Add the water or stock, salt and peppercorns. Bring to boil, reduce heat slightly and simmer, covered, slowly for 2¹/₂–3 hours.
3 ～Cool slightly, then strain mixture; remove the meat from bones and return meat to soup in pan. Discard the remaining solids.
4 ～Add onion, celery, potato and barley to soup mixture. Simmer, covered, for another 30 minutes, or until vegetables and barley are tender. Garnish with parsley, if desired.

Cock-a-leekie (top) and Oxtail Soup

∼ Stocks ∼

The secret to a great soup is good stock. Making it from scratch can sound daunting, but it couldn't be easier. It is also cheap and nutritious. Although a long cooking time is usually required, preparation is quick and the simmering pot needs scant attention on the stove. For beef and chicken stock, brown the bones before simmering to add flavour and colour, or use the remnants of a roast dinner. A fresh bouquet garni, made from large sprigs of parsley, thyme and a dried bay leaf tied in muslin, is preferable to the dried purchased version, but this can be substituted. Make double the amount of home-made stock and keep some on hand in the freezer. Stock should never be boiled. Heat slowly to boiling point, then reduce the heat—it should just simmer gently at all times.

Beef Stock

Preparation time:
20 minutes
Total cooking time:
4 hours 50 minutes

Makes 1 litre

2 kg beef bones	3 litres water
2 medium carrots, roughly chopped	2 sticks celery, leaves included, roughly chopped
2 medium brown onions, skins included, roughly chopped	1 bouquet garni
	12 black peppercorns

1 ∼Preheat oven to moderately hot 210°C. Place beef bones in a large baking dish and bake for 30 minutes, turning occasionally. Add the carrot and onion to dish and cook for another 20 minutes.
2 ∼Transfer the bones, carrot and onions to a large pan or stockpot. Drain excess fat from the baking dish then pour 1 cup of the water into the dish. Stir with a wooden spoon to dissolve any pan juices; add liquid to the pan or stockpot .

3 ∼Add celery, remaining water, bouquet garni and peppercorns to pan. Bring slowly to the boil, reduce heat and simmer, uncovered, for 4 hours. Skim froth from top of stock if necessary.

Strain stock through a fine sieve; discard the bones and vegetables. Cool quickly, then refrigerate until completely cold. Remove any fat that has set on the top.

Fish Stock

Preparation time:
15 minutes
Total cooking time:
30 minutes

Makes 1.5 litres

15 g butter	1.5 kg fish bones, heads
2 medium onions, finely	and tails
chopped	10 black peppercorns
2 litres water	1 bouquet garni

1 ⁓ Melt butter in a large pan and add onion. Cook, stirring, over low heat for 10 minutes until onion is soft and transparent. Do not allow to brown.
2 ⁓ Add water, fish bones, heads and tails, peppercorns and bouquet garni and bring slowly to the boil. Reduce heat and simmer, uncovered, for 20 minutes, frequently skimming any froth from the surface. Strain through a fine sieve, discard bones and vegetables and cool.
Note ⁓ Use a white-fleshed fish for stock. Darker-fleshed, oily fish may make stock greasy.

Chicken Stock

Preparation time:
20 minutes
Total cooking time:
3 hours 50 minutes

Makes 1.5 litres

1.5 kg chicken bones	2 sticks celery, leaves
2 large onions,	included, roughly
including skins,	chopped
roughly chopped	1 bouquet garni
3 litres water	12 black or white
2 medium carrots,	peppercorns
roughly chopped	

1 ⁓ Preheat oven to moderate 180°C. Place chicken bones and onion in large baking dish. Bake 50 minutes or until bones and onion are well browned. Transfer the bones and onion to a large pan or stockpot.
2 ⁓ Add the water, vegetables, bouquet garni and peppercorns to pan. Bring slowly to the boil, reduce heat and simmer, uncovered, for 3 hours, skimming froth from the top of stock if necessary. Strain stock through a fine sieve, discard solids.
3 ⁓ Cool stock quickly, then refrigerate until completely cold. Remove any fat that has set on the top.

~ Index ~